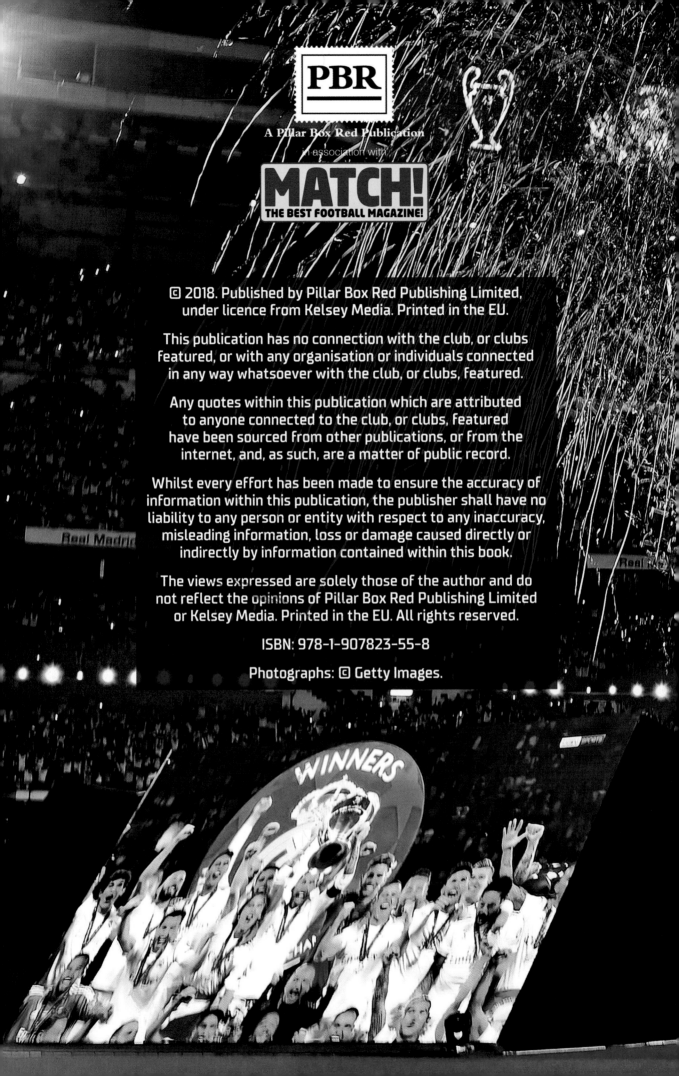

REAL MADRID ANNUAL 2019

Written by
Jamie Evans

Edited by
Stephen Fishlock

Designed by
Darryl Tooth

CONTENTS

SEASON REVIEW

We look back at Real's 2017-18 campaign month by month, checking out their key moments, star players and more!

AUGUST

MEGA MOMENTS!

Casemiro bags against Man. United

Real Madrid kicked off the 2017-18 season by lifting the UEFA Super Cup in Skopje, Macedonia against Man. United. Goals from midfielders Casemiro and Isco fired them to victory for the second time in a row, and their fourth European Super Cup in total!

Ronaldo is sent for an early bath

The first Clasico of the season took place at the Nou Camp for the Spanish Super Cup, and Real stunned Barça with a 3-1 win. Cristiano Ronaldo was heavily involved – scoring once before being sent off two minutes later for a second bookable offence – as Real made their first big statement of the season.

Three days later, Barcelona came to the Bernabeu for the second leg, but their hopes of a comeback were dashed within just four minutes, when Marco Asensio lashed an absolute screamer into the top corner! Another goal from striker Karim Benzema just before half-time sealed the victory, as Real won the trophy for the first time since 2012!

The players pose with their silverware

MAN OF THE MONTH!

MARCO ASENSIO The young starlet announced himself as a Real star with goals against Barcelona in both legs of the Super Cup. With Ronaldo banned for the opening league games too, somebody needed to stand up – and Asensio did big-time with two strikes against Valencia at the end of the month!

DID YOU KNOW?

Asensio's class goals against Barcelona meant that the wonderkid has scored on his La Liga, Copa del Rey, Champions League, European Super Cup and Spanish Super Cup debuts for Real. What a legend!

REAL'S RESULTS

Date	Comp	Home	Score	Away
08/08	USC	Real Madrid	2-1	Man. United
13/08	SUC	Barcelona	1-3	Real Madrid
16/08	SUC	Real Madrid	2-0	Barcelona
20/08	LIGA	Deportivo	0-3	Real Madrid
27/08	LIGA	Real Madrid	2-2	Valencia

SEPTEMBER

MEGA MOMENTS!

CR7 is spot on from 12 yards

Real kicked off the defence of their Champo League trophy with an easy victory against APOEL. Ronaldo opened the scoring before adding a second from the spot – breaking the record for penalties scored in the competition, as well as most home CL goals!

REAL'S RESULTS

09/09	LIGA	Real Madrid	1-1	Levante
13/09	UCL	Real Madrid	3-0	APOEL
17/09	LIGA	Real Sociedad	1-3	Real Madrid
20/09	LIGA	Real Madrid	0-1	Real Betis
23/09	LIGA	Alaves	1-2	Real Madrid
26/09	UCL	B. Dortmund	1-3	Real Madrid

Bale puts on the burners

When Real visited Sociedad, Gareth Bale had the supporters remembering his famous goal against Barça in the 2014 Copa del Rey final. The Welshman destroyed his marker with a phenomenal burst of pace, before chipping the ball over the keeper!

MAN OF THE MONTH!

DANI CEBALLOS The new boy made a big impact in his first start for Los Blancos, bagging two goals away to Alaves with a couple of top-class finishes!

DID YOU KNOW?

Ronaldo's goal against Cypriot champions APOEL was the sixth time in a row that he'd scored in the opening game of the Champions League. Wow!

OCTOBER

MEGA MOMENTS!

Ronaldo hammers it past Getafe

Real left it late in Getafe, but sealed a dramatic win thanks to Ronaldo. Los Blancos had been pegged back to 1-1 after Karim Benzema's brilliant opener, but when CR7 latched onto Isco's chipped ball in the 85th minute, there was only going to be one result!

REAL'S RESULTS

01/10	LIGA	Real Madrid	2-0	Espanyol
14/10	LIGA	Getafe	1-2	Real Madrid
17/10	UCL	Real Madrid	1-1	Tottenham
22/10	LIGA	Real Madrid	3-0	Eibar
26/10	CDR	Fuenlabrada	0-2	Real Madrid
29/10	LIGA	Girona	2-1	Real Madrid

Marcelo is mobbed by his team-mates

A brilliant goal from substitute Marcelo capped an easy win against Eibar. A beautiful move, starring a delicate flick from Benzema and a surging run from Theo Hernandez, was finished emphatically from the edge of the box by the Brazilian's left foot!

MAN OF THE MONTH!

ISCO The silky midfielder hit top form in October. He kicked off the month with an ace match-winning brace against Espanyol, scored and created another on international duty for Spain, before bagging more assists against Getafe and Eibar and yet another goal at Girona. He was absolutely on flames!

DID YOU KNOW?

Real Madrid's 1-1 draw at home to Tottenham stretched their unbeaten run in the Champions League group stage to 30 matches. Incredible!

NOVEMBER

MEGA MOMENTS!

Asensio struck arguably Real's La Liga goal of the season in the home victory over Las Palmas – either side of efforts by Casemiro and Isco. When the ball bounced to him 25 yards out, he hit an absolute bullet with his left foot straight into the top corner, giving the keeper no chance!

Wondergoal alert by Asensio

Nacho is pumped after his goal

Real Madrid bounced back from a really disappointing Champions League result at Wembley against Spurs with an absolutely devastating display in Cyprus! Ronaldo and Benzema both scored twice against APOEL, with Nacho and Luka Modric adding the others, to bag second spot in the group and reach the CL knockout stages for the 21st year in a row!

REAL'S RESULTS

01/11	UCL	Tottenham	3-1	Real Madrid
05/11	LIGA	Real Madrid	3-0	Las Palmas
18/11	LIGA	Atletico Madrid	0-0	Real Madrid
21/11	UCL	APOEL	0-6	Real Madrid
25/11	LIGA	Real Madrid	3-2	Malaga
28/11	CDR	Real Madrid	2-2	Fuenlabrada

MAN OF THE MONTH!

CASEMIRO The Brazilian was at his defensive best to help guide his team to a valuable point in the first Madrid derby at Atletico's new stadium, and also bagged two rare goals v Malaga and Las Palmas!

DID YOU KNOW?

Ronaldo's goal against Tottenham was his 10th against the North London club in all competitions – that's more than against any other English side!

DECEMBER

MEGA MOMENTS!

C-Ron nets

Real were on fire against Sevilla! They were only above the CL-chasers on goal difference before the clash, but ran out 5-0 winners – with all five goals coming in the first half! Defender Nacho scored again, and Cristiano Ronaldo doubled his La Liga goal tally for the season by grabbing a brilliant brace!

UAE side Al Jazira gave Real a big fright in the FIFA Club World Cup semi-finals, leading 1-0 at half-time. But Los Blancos bounced back. Ronaldo equalised thanks to a Modric assist, before Bale came off the bench to bag the winner!

Super sub Bale

2017 ended in the best way possible, with more silverware added to the trophy cabinet. A 25-yard free-kick from Ronaldo was enough for victory against Brazilian side Gremio, as Real became the first team to win back-to-back Club World Cups.

Trophy time for Real

REAL'S RESULTS

02/12	LIGA	Athletic Bilbao	0-0	Real Madrid
06/12	UCL	Real Madrid	3-2	B. Dortmund
09/12	LIGA	Real Madrid	5-0	Sevilla
13/12	FCW	Al Jazira	1-2	Real Madrid
16/12	FCW	Real Madrid	1-0	Gremio
23/12	LIGA	Real Madrid	0-3	Barcelona

MAN OF THE MONTH!

CRISTIANO RONALDO Ronaldo celebrated his fifth Ballon d'Or with five goals, inspiring his team to the Club World Cup, and becoming the first player to net in every single Champo League group stage game!

DID YOU KNOW?

Toni Kroos and Cristiano Ronaldo are the only players in history to have won four FIFA Club World Cups!

JANUARY

MEGA MOMENTS!

Braces for Nacho, Ronaldo and Bale helped Real to their biggest win of the season against Deportivo, but the Wales wizard provided the highlight. Collecting a cross on the right side of the penalty area, the winger shifted the ball onto his left foot and curled a wicked shot into the top corner!

Bale and Nacho embrace

Kroos buries a screamer

A ruthless attacking display at Valencia was capped in style by a brilliant goal from Toni Kroos. After a neat one-two on the edge of the box with Mateo Kovacic, the Germany midfielder swept the ball into the bottom corner to seal a brilliant result!

REAL'S RESULTS

Date	Comp	Home	Score	Away
04/01	CDR	Numancia	0-3	Real Madrid
07/01	LIGA	Celta Vigo	2-2	Real Madrid
10/01	CDR	Real Madrid	2-2	Numancia
13/01	LIGA	Real Madrid	0-1	Villarreal
18/01	CDR	Leganes	0-1	Real Madrid
21/01	LIGA	Real Madrid	7-1	Deportivo
24/01	CDR	Real Madrid	1-2	Leganes
27/01	LIGA	Valencia	1-4	Real Madrid

MAN OF THE MONTH!

TONI KROOS Real Madrid's superstar attackers hogged the credit for their big January wins, but they couldn't have done it without the excellent Kroos. The German produced a brilliant passing display to dominate Valencia's midfield, and bagged assists against both Celta Vigo and Deportivo.

DID YOU KNOW?

The 7-1 thrashing of Deportivo was the sixth time since 2010 that Real Madrid had scored five or more goals against The Blues and Whites!

FEBRUARY

MEGA MOMENTS!

Ron loves the Champo League

Real had a tough draw in the Champo League last 16, and there were plenty of nerves when Adrien Rabiot put PSG in front. But when CR7 scored for the eighth CL game in a row, the tide turned. The No.7 added a second, before Marcelo made it safe with number three!

One of the highest scoring games of the La Liga season produced lots of drama and comebacks! Betis recovered from an Asensio opener to lead 2-1 before half-time, but Real roared back in the second half to make it 4-2. A late goal from the home side led to a nervy finish, until Benzema sealed the three points in stoppage-time!

Benzema bags

Casemiro jumps for joy

Casemiro equalled the best scoring season of his league career in style at Leganes. Benzema was instrumental in the goal, dropping deep to link up with the Brazilian and creating space for him to run into the box, before finishing off the ace move!

MAN OF THE MONTH!

SERGIO RAMOS He comes alive in the CL knockout games and did a great job marshalling Real's defence against Neymar, Cavani and Mbappe. February was a top month for him in attack too, with three goals!

DID YOU KNOW?

Lucas Vazquez's opener v Real Sociedad came after just 48 seconds – Real's fastest goal of the season!

REAL'S RESULTS

Date	Comp	Home	Score	Away
03/02	LIGA	Levante	2-2	Real Madrid
10/02	LIGA	Real Madrid	5-2	Real Sociedad
14/02	UCL	Real Madrid	3-1	PSG
18/02	LIGA	Real Betis	3-5	Real Madrid
21/02	LIGA	Leganes	1-3	Real Madrid
24/02	LIGA	Real Madrid	4-0	Alaves
27/02	LIGA	Espanyol	1-0	Real Madrid

MARCH

MEGA MOMENTS!

Another Champions League goal for Cristiano Ronaldo against PSG – a thumping header – meant Real Madrid had one foot in the last eight, before a red card for midfielder Marco Verratti put the result beyond any doubt. Edinson Cavani's lucky goal was cancelled out by Casemiro's deflected effort, meaning Real had reached the CL quarter-finals for the eighth consecutive season!

Ron's the man yet again

More celebrations from Cristiano

Exactly a month after the crazy goal-fest in Betis, Real Madrid produced another high-scoring classic at home to Girona. Ronaldo stole the show again with four goals, including the 50th hat-trick of his career, as he tore the opposition defence to pieces!

MAN OF THE MONTH!

CRISTIANO RONALDO Scoring in every single game he played for Real in March made it another memorable month for CR7! Wicked braces against Getafe and Eibar, plus a four-goal haul at home to Girona, meant that the deadly Portugal legend had scored 21 goals in his last 11 matches. Amazing!

DID YOU KNOW?

Against PSG, Karim Benzema became only the third Frenchman in history to play 100 Champions League games, after Thierry Henry and Patrice Evra!

REAL'S RESULTS

03/03	LIGA	Real Madrid	3-1	Getafe
06/03	UCL	PSG	1-2	Real Madrid
10/03	LIGA	Eibar	1-2	Real Madrid
18/03	LIGA	Real Madrid	6-3	Girona
31/03	LIGA	Las Palmas	0-3	Real Madrid

APRIL

MEGA MOMENTS!

CR7's epic wondergoal

The CL quarter-final between Juventus and Real featured two huge clubs, legendary players and A-list managers, but it'll be remembered for Ronaldo's bicycle-kick! The acrobatic finish gave goalkeeper Gianluigi Buffon no chance, and Real their first win in Turin for 56 years!

The second leg proved even more dramatic than the first! Juve's comeback to lead 3-0 in Madrid stunned Real, and extra-time looked a certainty until the 93rd minute, when Medhi Benatia conceded a clumsy penalty. In the protests, Buffon was sent off, but Ronaldo kept his cool to fire Real to the semis!

Real make it to the semis

Marcelo celebrates

The CL semi-final draw meant Real would have to reach the final the hard way – by beating the French, Italian and German champs. Marcelo and Asensio provided the vital away goals in a 2-1 win over Bayern, but the tie was far from over.

MAN OF THE MONTH!

CRISTIANO RONALDO His Turin screamer should have been enough to make him star man alone, but he added goals in the Madrid derby, in the second leg v Juve and with a late equaliser against Athletic Bilbao!

DID YOU KNOW?

Real's win over Juve meant they'd reached the Champo League semi-finals for a record eighth year in a row!

REAL'S RESULTS

03/04	UCL	Juventus	0-3	Real Madrid
08/04	LIGA	Real Madrid	1-1	Atletico Madrid
11/04	UCL	Real Madrid	1-3	Juventus
15/04	LIGA	Malaga	1-2	Real Madrid
18/04	LIGA	Real Madrid	1-1	Athletic Bilbao
25/04	UCL	Bayern Munich	1-2	Real Madrid
28/04	LIGA	Real Madrid	2-1	Leganes

Bale scores one of the greatest CL final goals of all time

MAY

MEGA MOMENTS!

Navas makes one of eight saves v Bayern

After 63 minutes of the CL semi-final second leg against Bayern, Bernabeu bosses must have been having serious regrets. James Rodriguez, on loan from Real, had just scored to make it 2-2, and the momentum was with the Germans. But thanks to some brave defending and top saves from Keylor Navas, Los Blancos held on to reach another final.

Bale and Ronaldo high-five

Although Real Madrid were out of the La Liga title race for their visit to Barcelona, no Clasico can ever be taken lightly! They fell behind twice, but Ronaldo and Bale both bagged brilliant goals to secure a 2-2 draw at the home of their biggest enemies!

CL trophy number 13 for Real

Winning one Champions League is magic enough, but winning three in a row is historic. Although they had a big helping hand from goalkeeper Loris Karius for the first and third goals, Bale's phenomenal overhead-kick was worthy of winning any game!

MAN OF THE MONTH!

GARETH BALE After scoring against Barça, Celta Vigo and Villarreal, Bale was unlucky to be left out of the CL final, but he still had a big impact on the game as a sub. His epic bicycle-kick rivalled both Ronaldo's effort in the quarters and Zinedine Zidane's volley in the 2001 final as Real's greatest ever CL goal, and ensured that 2018 will be remembered as his final!

DID YOU KNOW?

Real became the first team to win two Champions League finals with exactly the same starting line-up!

REAL'S RESULTS

01/05	UCL	Real Madrid	2-2	Bayern Munich
06/05	LIGA	Barcelona	2-2	Real Madrid
09/05	LIGA	Sevilla	3-2	Real Madrid
12/05	LIGA	Real Madrid	6-0	Celta Vigo
19/05	LIGA	Villarreal	2-2	Real Madrid
26/05	UCL	Real Madrid	3-1	Liverpool

CHAMPIONS

In May 2018, Real Madrid celebrated lifting their 13th Champions League trophy! Check out the numbers behind their record win...

3 They are the first team to win it three times in a row since Bayern Munich in the 1970s!

2 Gareth Bale became the first substitute ever to score twice in a Champions League final!

13 It was Real Madrid's 13th victory in the competition – six more than nearest rivals AC Milan. Wow!

11 Real won the trophy in 2018 with exactly the same starting line-up as the 2017 final!

REAL MADRID	**3-1**	**LIVERPOOL**
Benzema 51; Bale 64, 83		Mane 55

A moment of magic from Wales legend Gareth Bale was sandwiched between two moments of absolute madness from Liverpool keeper Loris Karius! The German goalie practically handed the ball to Real striker Karim Benzema for the opener, but there was nothing he could do about Bale's jaw-dropping bicycle-kick, which restored Real's lead after Sadio Mane's equaliser. It was one of the greatest goals in Champions League final history, and when the Welshman's long-range shot was flapped by GK Karius to make it 3-1, trophy number 13 was sealed!

1 Zinedine Zidane became the first manager ever to win three CLs in a row – only two other gaffers have won three in their entire careers!

5 Cristiano Ronaldo overtook CL legends Andres Iniesta and Clarence Seedorf to lift his fifth Champions League trophy!

The wordsearch was to easy! Just like my hand writing

WORDSEARCH

Can you find these Champo League-winning Real Madrid stars?

```
F A L O P E Z O C Y W Y S M G E Y A V I Z V U T R L D G S K
A O Z C L Z N S N M V Q P Z S W J Q S I E Y K Z R V G I D U
U U Q P H Q M G V H M R Q K U O H F F G O B H C E M Q O D R
Q S S H H I Z P Q R H C C L K S H A X R D A M J I H R Z M L
S W V K Y D R B C S D K M J E G H C R J D A W F Z I Q A K P
H U J I R W M S M R B W I A R Y I A Q O T R Z Z M H D W O X
A R B E L O A Q K E U B F W N R V Z V A K X X E C R K O V X
I E S O R U X D G D E I S G D A J X R W M S C P D N A C U
Q B D A R X R U E F N R F O N L M O D B H A G V V J D N V H
W F T A W T Y O N C O V M H D H M A L I C Q Z H Q I U E M I
U S Z R C F S D T W J E V O I F H G N M Z G O K B Q O L E Y
H O N V S Z I T O N Q W K R E C W J T C M G H S H E Z K I M
J F L B H Y M U R T E B A Z Y T A M Y D B Q T Z S V D A V V
N Z I S Y Z J H M B R L R M A K E L E L E X Y T E I C D S D
G K P Q A P P D I H O U I I F D W C L M P T S N E L Z S U L
H X A R K P W S M S O F J C Q Q N R H M E Q H K D L P G F Z
A W M Q O F F C A G H R O B N H J F E C P D P E O A C W R G
T P I F V W I P P A N F T V E F S K W D E O Y J R R H T P M
N I U C R S O A L P B P W G C I P A W L O M W I F R K F Z Q
S G P S N K E T I C X I X R R G H R T T O N V H N A O Y W J
K H F S K U U X S N O W D K C O S A S T H Q D L A M S E V L
W Q Y Y W A D F D W S A V V H O V N U X T O J O S E I T O T
W J P M I R S F Y W G X O M O I Q K T H L P A V O N A C A N
V H H F E L N V E A F A T R I Z E A K I I G L B Y D L J G N
N O I M S G Z R R E T F K I G Y A R N Y Y G O T D I U R W N
C O N P Y Y B R W O W B H T E J E A R J K I Z Z H E E B I F
W R Z I Q W A B R E F P Z V V Q D Y R O Y O J J W E O T P S
F H D Y O Z T A B N E L H K T X J F U T Y K H E D I R A S Z
W K C X A W S K G U T I E G F A Z L J W U C A C W S P A V Z
L W N X L G B X D U S X M O B I N M O R I E N T E S S R T K
```

Anelka	Gento	Khedira	Modric	Puskas
Arbeloa	Guti	Kopa	Morata	Redondo
Bueno	Hierro	Kroos	Morientes	Seedorf
Casemiro	Illarramendi	Lopez	Navarro	Solari
Danilo	Joseito	Makelele	Pavon	Suker
Figo	Karanka	McManaman	Pepe	Zarraga

NAME THE TEAM

Real's 2017–18 season began with their UEFA Super Cup victory over Man. United! Can you remember their starting line-up?

1. Goalkeeper
keylor navas

2. Centre-back
sergio ramos

3. Midfielder
Toni kros

4. Defensive midfielder
casemiro

5. Forward
Karim Benzima

6. Centre-back
Rafeal varane

7. Forward
gareth bale

8. Left-back
marcelo

9. Right-back
Dani carvival

10. Attacking midfielder
isco

11. Midfielder
Luka modric

ANSWERS ON PAGE 60

THE BERNABEU IN NUMBERS

Here's everything you need to know about Real's enormous stadium!

1947
The year the massive stadium was built!

1957
Real won their second European Cup on their home ground in 1957!

35
It's named after Santiago Bernabeu, who was Real Madrid president for 35 years!

81,044

That's the current capacity, which makes it the second biggest stadium in Spain!

130,00

The Bernabeu's record attendance – in 1962 v Juventus in the European Cup!

1964

The ground hosted the Euro 1964 final when Spain beat Soviet Union 2–1!

6

The famous ground is the sixth biggest football stadium in Europe!

4

Four Champions League finals have been played there – only Wembley has hosted more!

1982

In 1982, it became the first European stadium to host a Euros and World Cup final!

ISCO

THE MAGIC MAN

The magician is ready to become Real Madrid and Spain's main man.

When Real Madrid need somebody to conjure something out of nothing, Isco is the man that they usually turn to. Since joining the Spanish giants from Malaga in 2013, he's registered tons of assists and a number of goals, but he's about more than just stats. The attacking midfielder has a level of creativity and flair that very few players can match, and that's what makes him such a joy to watch. His ability to drift past players as if they're not there and his eagle-eyed vision to spot a pass make him a huge threat, whether he's playing out wide or in the middle. Like so many of Real's big names, he's already got a huge collection of trophies and medals, and looks set to add to them for years to come. With Cristiano Ronaldo now a former player at the Bernabeu, Isco is ready to pick up the mantle as Real Madrid's No.1 star!

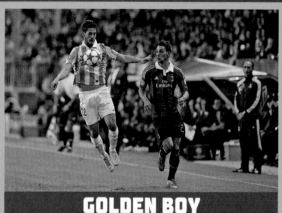

GOLDEN BOY

Isco made his name at Malaga after joining from Valencia in 2011. In his first season, he got five goals and four assists to help them qualify for the Champo League for the first time in their history, allowing him to take his talent to the highest level. With three goals and three assists, he was the star of their run to the CL quarter-finals, and earned the 2012 Golden Boy award for Europe's best young player.

EUROPE'S MOST WANTED

Many of Europe's biggest clubs were on red alert after his Champions League performances, and even more teams wanted to sign him after he inspired Spain to U21 European Championship glory in the summer of 2013. But there was only one club for him and when Real agreed to pay Malaga £23 million, the deal was done. Carlo Ancelotti's first signing was ready for the big time.

THE BREAKTHROUGH

At times, life at the Bernabeu has been tough for Isco. Competing for places with some of the best players in the world means he's struggled to find the right role and been shifted around positions. But in 2017, that changed. Given a run in his favourite CAM role, the Spaniard found his form, became a key player for the team and ended the season with La Liga and CL winners' medals.

SPAIN'S NEXT STAR

Isco is already one of the best creative midfielders in the world, but the next two years could see him become the main man for club and country. Cristiano Ronaldo's exit has given him the freedom to dictate Real's attacks, and he has the talent to replace Andres Iniesta as Spain's main playmaker too – indeed, he was La Roja's best player at World Cup 2018. The magician is ready to take over!

TROPHY CABINET

- **4x** Champions Leagues
- **1x** La Liga
- **3x** Club World Cups
- **1x** Copa del Rey
- **3x** European Super Cups
- **1x** Spanish Super Cup

RONALDO
450 GOALS

CRISTIANO RONALDO ensured he ended his career with Real Madrid in 2018 as a proper legend – by reaching the milestone of 450 goals!

GOAL
1

Real Madrid	3	2	Deportivo

August, 2009 Ronaldo opened his account for Real on his La Liga debut! He netted a well-struck penalty into the bottom corner to seal the win for his new team!

GOAL 7

Real Madrid 2 | 0 **Villarreal**

September, 2009 Cristiano was breaking records within a month of moving to the Bernabeu! By scoring against Villarreal, he became the first player in Real's history to score in all four of his first La Liga matches!

GOAL 50

Ajax 0 | 4 **Real Madrid**

November, 2010 After just over a year in Spain, Cristiano reached a half-century of goals for Madrid – an absolutely thumping effort in Amsterdam fired his team into the Champions League knockout stages!

GOAL 75

Barcelona 0 | 1 **Real Madrid**

April, 2011 He had to wait until his second season, but Ron got his hands on his first trophy in the Copa del Rey final. With the game in extra-time, CR7 met an Angel Di Maria cross with a towering header to bag the cup!

GOAL 100

Lyon 0 | 2 **Real Madrid**

November, 2011 Ronaldo reached his next massive milestone from the penalty spot in the Champo League. His second goal of the game in France against Lyon ensured Real's 100% record in the group stage!

GOAL '130

Real Madrid 5 | 1 Real Sociedad

March, 2012 It only took 92 matches for Ronaldo to reach 100 La Liga goals, breaking the previous club record held by Ferenc Puskas! He was deadly in front of goal, slotting coolly past the Sociedad goalkeeper!

GOAL '177

GOAL '178

GOAL '179

Real Madrid 4 | 0 Getafe

January, 2013 A hat-trick was the perfect way to bag 300 goals in club football. Ron struck with his left foot, right foot and header to seal an easy win against Getafe!

GOAL 200

Real Madrid 6 | 2 Malaga

May, 2013 The double century came up in an unlikely way, with GK Willy Caballero handling a back-pass. Ron stepped up to smash home the indirect free-kick from the six-yard box, and reach 200 goals in 197 matches!

GOAL 250

Bayern Munich 0 | 4 Real Madrid

April, 2014 This clever, drilled free-kick under the Bayern wall didn't just bring up the 250th goal for Ron, it also helped fire him to his first Champo League final for Real Madrid in his home country Portugal. Hero!

GOAL STATS!

Check out some of the epic numbers behind Ronaldo's scoring records...

7
Ronaldo is the FIFA Club World Cup's all-time top scorer with seven goals!

8
He shares the record for the most La Liga hat-tricks in a season!

50
He's the only player to score 50 goals in a calendar year seven times in a row!

Real Madrid 4 | 1 Atletico Madrid

May, 2014 In the final, Ronaldo bagged Real's fourth and final goal of the match from the penalty spot to seal his second CL trophy, and became the first player to score and win two finals with two different teams! No-one will ever forget his muscle man celebration!

GOAL 252

GOAL 279

GOAL 280

GOAL 281

Real Madrid 3 | 0 Celta Vigo

December, 2014 La Liga records kept on tumbling! Three more goals at the Bernabeu took Ronaldo past the league's previous hat-trick record of 23, and made him the quickest player ever to reach 200 goals in the competition's history – after just 178 games. Wow!

GOAL 300

Rayo Vallecano 0 | 2 Real Madrid

April, 2015 Goal number 300 was Cristiano at his predatory best. After a quality run and cross from Dani Carvajal, the legendary No.7 was on hand to power home an ace diving header from the edge of the six-yard box!

GOAL 314

GOAL 315

GOAL 316

GOAL 317

GOAL 318

Espanyol 0 | 6 Real Madrid

September, 2015 Ron opened his La Liga account for 2015-16 by matching his best ever tally of five goals in a match! In doing so, he also reached 230 league goals for Real – overtaking the previous record held by Raul!

61
His best season was in 2014-15, when he scored 61 times in all comps!

90
In 2014, he became the first player to score in every minute of a football match!

395
Ronaldo has scored more goals in Europe's top five leagues than any other player!

Cristiano Ronaldo
Bota de Oro

GOAL 324

Real Madrid 3 | 0 Levante

October 2015 A month later, Ronaldo caught Raul's other record too. His drilled finish at home to Levante made him Real Madrid's all-time top scorer, completing the feat in 431 games fewer than the ex-Spain striker!

GOAL 349

GOAL 350

GOAL 351

GOAL 352

Real Madrid 7 | 1 Celta Vigo

March, 2016 This four-goal haul featured some absolutely stunning strikes. First, Ronaldo opened the scoring with a wicked, dipping shot from 30 yards, then followed it up with an unstoppable free-kick! By adding two more, he moved to second on the list of all-time La Liga top scorers behind mega rival Lionel Messi!

GOAL 372

GOAL 373

GOAL 374

Atletico Madrid 0 | 3 Real Madrid

November, 2016 By bagging an ace hat-trick at the last ever La Liga Madrid derby at the Vicente Calderon, Ronaldo became the top goalscorer in the history of the clash, overtaking club legend Alfredo Di Stefano!

GOAL 393

GOAL 394

GOAL 395

Real Madrid 4 | 2 Bayern Munich

April, 2017 Lionel Messi and Ronaldo have spent most of their careers neck-and-neck in the CL scoring charts, but Cristiano beat his old rival to become the first player to score a century in the competition! He did it in style too, with a hat-trick in the 2017 semi-finals!

GOAL STATS!

Here's the breakdown of Ronaldo's 450-goal haul during his epic Real Madrid career!

HOW?
- 32 Free-kicks
- 79 Penalties
- 339 Open Play

WHEN?
- 6 Extra Time
- 203 First Half
- 241 Second Half

POSITION?
- 93 Centre Forward
- 6 Right Wing
- 351 Left Wing

COMPETITION?
- 4 SSC*
- 2 USC*
- 6 FCWC*
- 311 La Liga
- 22 CDR*
- 105 Champions League

*Key: CDR = Copa del Rey; FCWC = FIFA Club World Cup; SSC = Spanish Super Cup; USC = UEFA Super Cup

Real Madrid 4 | 1 Sevilla

May, 2017 There aren't many players who score 400 goals for one club! This was just a tap-in, but showed why Ronaldo is still going so strong – his mega deadly instincts and lethal finishing skills are super dangerous!

GOAL
400

GOAL
449

Barcelona 2 | 2 Real Madrid

May, 2018 It wasn't enough to stop Barcelona from winning the league, but Ronaldo's close-range finish at the Nou Camp made him Real Madrid's joint top scorer in El Clasico history, tied with Di Stefano on 18 goals!

GOAL
450

Villarreal 2 | 2 Real Madrid

May, 2018 Ronaldo left it to the last day of the La Liga season, but he did finally bag goal number 450 with a header. He'll forever be remembered as a Real Madrid legend, and probably their greatest player of all time!

OPPOSITION?
- 18 Barcelona
- 27 Sevilla
- 20 Celta Vigo
- 22 Atletico Madrid
- 23 Getafe

GOALKEEPER?
- 12 Sergio Alvarez
- 15 Gorka Iraizoz
- 12 Ruben Martinez
- 12 Claudio Bravo
- 13 Javi Varas

ASSISTED BY?
- 31 Mesut Ozil
- 47 Karim Benzema
- 32 Gareth Bale

MANAGER?
- 25 Benitez
- 33 Pellegrini
- 168 Mourinho
- 112 Zidane
- 112 Ancelotti

BEST SEASON?
- 54 2010-11
- 61 2014-15
- 55 2012-13
- 60 2011-12

REAL ST

KROOS

After spending the summer of 2014 putting chances on a plate for his Germany team-mates at the World Cup, Toni Kroos was nicknamed 'The Waiter!'

BENZEMA

Karim has eight siblings in total and two of his younger brothers – Gressy and Sabri – are also footballers at amateur level!

MARCELO

The Brazilian is a Madrid hero, but he's really a fan of Botafogo in Brazil and wants to end his career with the team from Rio de Janeiro!

ASENSIO

Marco has been nicknamed 'Torero' by his team-mates, which means bullfighter. But it's not because he's brave – Dani Carvajal reckons he looks like a famous matador!

VARANE

Zinedine Zidane called Raphael Varane to convince him to sign for Real, but the young defender asked him to call back as he was revising for an exam!

HERNANDEZ

Theo's dad Jean-Francois played for Real Madrid's rivals Atletico in 2000-01, and his older brother Lucas plays for Atletico now!

ARS revealed!

BALE

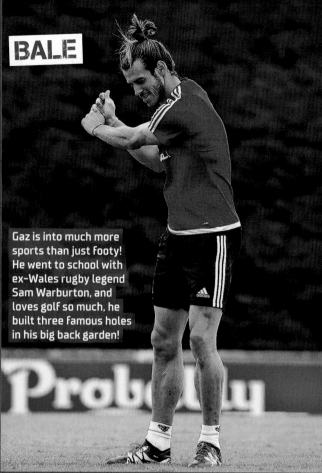

Gaz is into much more sports than just footy! He went to school with ex-Wales rugby legend Sam Warburton, and loves golf so much, he built three famous holes in his big back garden!

NAVAS

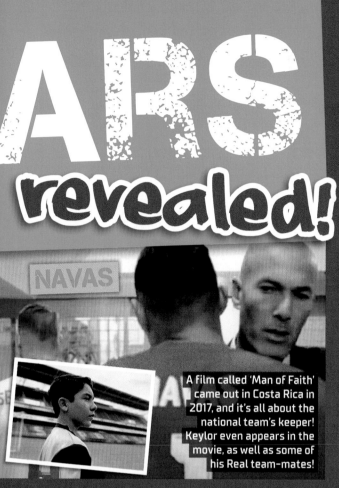

A film called 'Man of Faith' came out in Costa Rica in 2017, and it's all about the national team's keeper! Keylor even appears in the movie, as well as some of his Real team-mates!

NACHO

Nacho's little brother Alex is a footballer too, and the pair of them came through the Real Madrid academy together!

RAMOS

Sergio is a multi-talented man. Off the pitch, the tough defender is handy with a guitar, and released an ace rap single called 'SR4' ahead of the 2018 Champions League final!

ISCO

At Real, Isco is known as 'The Magic Kid', but when he played for Malaga his team-mates called him 'El Culon' – The Big Bum!

ODRIOZOLA

The new boy comes from a sporty family. One of his cousins is a professional handball player, and his uncle runs a Spanish basketball team in San Sebastian!

MODRIC

As a kid, Modric was given a pair of Nike shinpads with his footy idol Ronaldo on them. Luka loved the shinnies so much, he wore them right up until turning pro!

REAL MADRID BRAIN-BUSTER!

How well do you know the Spanish giants?

1. What year was the club founded – 1898, 1900 or 1902?

2. Which Spain midfielder scored the club's 6,000th goal in their history back in February?

3. What national team does Real Madrid goalkeeper Keylor Navas play for?

4. True or False? Real Madrid legend Raul started his career at mega rivals Barcelona!

5. Which goalkeeper has played more Champions League games for Real than any other player?

6. Who scored Real's late equaliser in their 2-2 draw with Barça at the Nou Camp in May?

7. Take Real's number of CL wins, and add it to Benzema's squad number – what have you got?

8. True or False? Zinedine Zidane was the world's most expensive player when he joined Real!

REAL MADRID CF

TOTTENHAM HOTSPUR FC

APOEL FC

9. In 2017-18, Real came through a CL group containing APOEL, Spurs and which German club?

ISCO 23

10. Which La Liga club did Real sign midfielder Isco from?

1 1902
2 asensio
3 costa rica
4 False False
5 Casielias
6 gareth bale
7 22
8 True
9 Borissia Dortmund
10 malaga

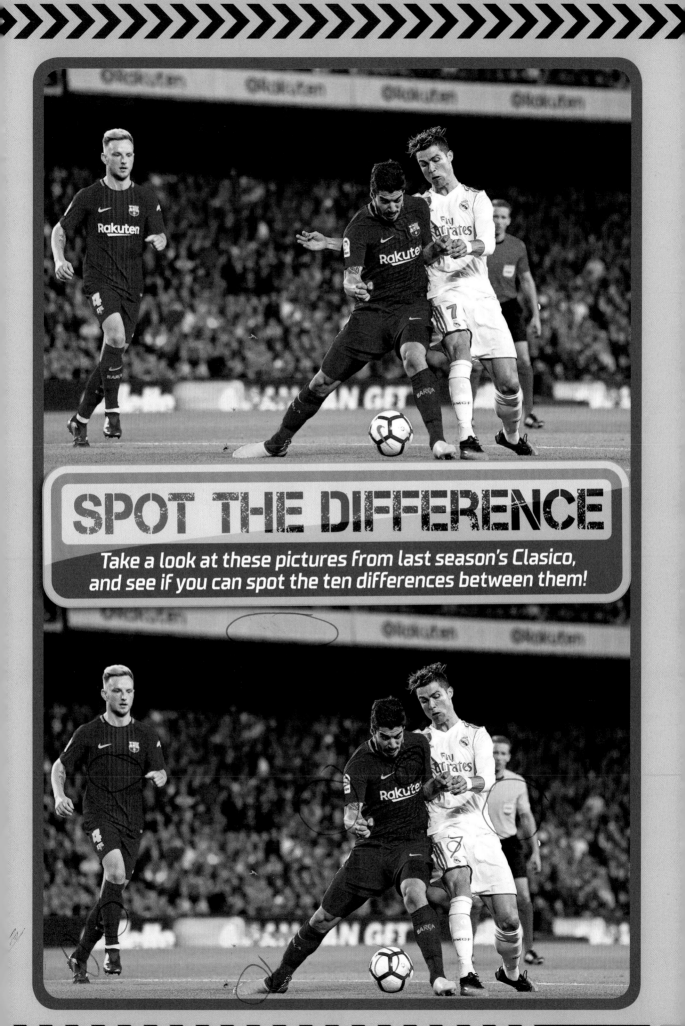

SPOT THE DIFFERENCE

Take a look at these pictures from last season's Clasico, and see if you can spot the ten differences between them!

ANSWERS ON PAGE 60

ASENSIO
STAR IN THE MAKING

Real Madrid young gun Marco Asensio is ready to rock 2018-19.

Many players go through their entire football careers without getting close to starring in a Champions League final, but Real Madrid's Marco Asensio has already played in two, scored in one and won both of them – and he's still in his early 20s! With a wand of a left foot, a rocket long shot and explosive turn of pace, the young Mallorcan-born midfielder is already well known as one of the most exciting players in European football. Indeed, he was the youngest player in Spain's 2018 World Cup squad which travelled to Russia last summer. Back in February 2018, the Spaniard also entered Real Madrid's history books after scoring the club's 6,000th goal in a match against Real Betis and, with his incredible talent, Asensio looks set to play a massive role in both Real Madrid and the Spanish national team's futures.

MALLORCA WONDERKID

Asensio caught the eye before even kicking a ball in senior footy. The youngster's displays in Mallorca's academy had Real and Barça battling it out to sign him when he was a teenager, but he stayed with his hometown club and by 2014 was a regular in the Segunda Division. Real were waiting and in December 2014 they agreed a £3.5 million deal, allowing him to stay in Palma until the summer.

THE NEW GALACTICOS

The biggest names are always linked with Real, but the signing of Asensio was different. The club realised that given time, he had the potential to be just as good as any of their record-breaking transfers. He was sent out on loan to La Liga side Espanyol, where he registered four goals and ten assists – more than any other under-21 star in the country. When he came back, he was ready for Real.

SUPER CUP SUPERSTAR

On his return, Marco wasted no time in making his impact. When the ball fell to him 25 yards from goal in the UEFA Super Cup clash with Sevilla, he didn't think twice before whipping the ball into the top corner with his left foot – and it's a sight that Madrid fans have got used to. In the Spanish Super Cup a year later, he repeated the stunner not once but twice, this time against fierce rivals Barça.

NEXT IN LINE

Cristiano Ronaldo's departure means there's a chance for someone to become the new king of Madrid, and Asensio could be that man. At 22, he's already won the Champions League twice, netted in a final and hit tons of wondergoals along the way. If he continues to progress, Asensio could become an all-time Madrid great – not bad for a player that was more than 20 times cheaper than Cristiano.

#asensio

FACTPACK

Position: Att. midfielder

Country: Spain

D.O.B: 21/1/1996

Height: 6ft

Boots: Nike Mercurial Superfly

Instagram: @marcoasensio10

ALL-TIME
REAL MADRID

DREAM TEAM

Check out some of the Real Madrid greats, and pick who you'd want in an all-time XI for the chance to win an awesome prize!

DREAM TEAM
GOALKEEPERS!

JUAN ALONSO
SEASONS: 1949-63

The Madrid team that won five European Cups in the 1950s and '60s needed a legendary keeper, and Alonso was just that. 'Juanito' was key to Los Blancos' success, captaining the team in 1958, and is still the most successful GK in the history of the competition!

PACO BUYO
SEASONS: 1986-97

Real won six titles in 11 years with Buyo between the sticks and he became a huge fans' favourite after joining from Sevilla. He bagged two Zamora Trophies, and retired at Real with 542 La Liga appearances to his name – only three players have played more. What a total legend!

RICARDO ZAMORA
SEASONS: 1930-36

The reason the best keeper in La Liga is given the Zamora Trophy is because of this guy! The legendary shot-stopper played for Real in the 1930s, helping the club win two La Liga titles, and is still remembered as one of Spain's greatest ever GKs!

KEYLOR NAVAS
SEASONS: 2014-PRESENT

Real snapped up Navas after his displays at World Cup 2014 helped Costa Rica reach the last eight. In his first season he shared keeping duties with Iker Casillas, but then established himself as No.1, starting all of Real's last three CL victories!

IKER CASILLAS
SEASONS: 1999-2015

Casillas was 18 when he first broke into Real's first team and looked a legend in the making. He became the youngest GK to win a CL final and, by the time he left 16 years later, he'd lifted the trophy two more times and played over 500 club games!

BEST OF THE REST...
CHECK OUT THESE OTHER SUPERSTARS!

BODO ILLGNER
Seasons: 1996-2001

ROGELIO DOMINGUEZ
Seasons: 1957-62

SANTIAGO CANIZARES
Seasons: 1994-98

DIEGO LOPEZ
Seasons: 2005-07 & 13-14

NOW PICK YOUR ALL-TIME REAL MADRID DREAM TEAM GOALKEEPER!

TURN TO PAGE 42

DREAM TEAM
FULL-BACKS!

MARCELO

SEASONS: 2007-PRESENT

In 2007, Madrid headed to Brazil to try to find the next Roberto Carlos – and that's exactly what they got! Marcelo has pace, energy and the skill of a world-class winger, and he's played a key role in Real's last four Champions League wins!

ROBERTO CARLOS

SEASONS: 1996-2007

Snapping up Carlos from Inter was one of the best signings Real ever made! The Brazilian was one of the best attacking full-backs of all time, and had an absolutely rocket left foot! With 527 games, no foreign player has played more for Madrid!

MICHEL SALGADO

SEASONS: 1999-2009

Salgado owned Real's right wing during their Galactico years, and he was just as reliable joining in with attacks as he was in defence. In 371 games for Los Blancos, the right-back won two Champions Leagues and four La Ligas!

CHENDO

SEASONS: 1982-98

The one-club man was one of the most consistent in the history of Los Blancos, playing 497 games! The Madridistas absolutely loved Chendo, and he ended his career in style – by winning Real's seventh Champions League trophy!

JOSE ANTONIO CAMACHO

SEASONS: 1973-89

Camacho was a real wonderkid when he burst into Spain and Real's first teams, and stayed in both for years. The tough-tackling LB is seventh on Real's all-time appearance list with 577 games, and lifted the La Liga trophy an incredible nine times!

BEST OF THE REST... CHECK OUT THESE OTHER SUPERSTARS!

RAFAEL LESMES
Seasons: 1952-60

DANI CARVAJAL
Seasons: 2013-Present

GABRIEL HEINZE
Seasons: 2007-09

ALVARO ARBELOA
Seasons: 2004-06 & 09-16

NOW PICK YOUR ALL-TIME REAL MADRID DREAM TEAM FULL-BACKS!

TURN TO PAGE 42

DREAM TEAM
CENTRE-BACKS!

FERNANDO HIERRO

SEASONS: 1989-2003

Hierro was no ordinary CB – he was a real leader, a top-class passer and a proper goal threat. In 601 games for Real Madrid he scored 127 times from defence and, when he retired in 2003, he even led Spain's list of all-time top goalscorers. Bonkers!

FABIO CANNAVARO

SEASONS: 2006-09

The last defender to win the Ballon d'Or joined Madrid from Juventus after winning the 2006 World Cup as Italy skipper. Cannavaro guided Real to the 2007 and 2008 La Liga titles, and is considered one of the greatest centre-backs ever!

SERGIO RAMOS

SEASONS: 2005-PRESENT

Ramos might be a villain to refs and opposition fans, but his world-class defending and leadership have made him a massive hero to Madridistas! In 2018, he became the first player to start and win three Champions League finals as captain!

JOSE SANTAMARIA

SEASONS: 1957-66

The Uruguayan CB was one of the world's best defenders in the 1950s and '60s, and his presence allowed forwards Di Stefano and Puskas to attack at will. With Santamaria in defence, Real won four European Cups and six La Ligas. Legend!

MANUEL SANCHIS

SEASONS: 1983-2001

One of Real's most legendary captains watched his father play for the club, then went on to break the all-time appearance record himself! Sanchis was a classy defender, and ended his one-club career perfectly – by lifting the Champions League!

BEST OF THE REST...   CHECK OUT THESE OTHER SUPERSTARS!

IVAN HELGUERA
Seasons: 1999-2007

IVAN CAMPO
Seasons: 1998-2003

RAPHAEL VARANE
Seasons: 2011-Present

PEPE
Seasons: 2007-17

NOW PICK YOUR ALL-TIME REAL MADRID DREAM TEAM CENTRE-BACKS!

TURN TO PAGE 42

DREAM TEAM
MIDFIELDERS!

DAVID BECKHAM

SEASONS: 2003-07

Becks was the world's most famous player when he joined Real, but by the time he left he was one of their most important too. Ronaldo and Raul bagged tons of goals from his deliveries, and he was a hero in their dramatic La Liga win in 2006-07!

CLAUDE MAKELELE

SEASONS: 2000-03

If you want a quality defensive midfielder in your team, then this guy has to be the man! The France star was so good that his position in front of the back four became known as 'the Makelele role' throughout the world of footy!

CLARENCE SEEDORF

SEASONS: 1996-99

Seedorf was part of a golden generation of Dutch players that came through Ajax's youth academy in the early 1990s. He won La Liga and the CL with Madrid, and is still the only footballer ever to win the latter with three different clubs!

PIRRI

SEASONS: 1964-80

Pirri hit 172 goals for Real and won the European Cup, before moving into the defence. He was a proper warrior – he ended a European Cup Winners' Cup final with his arm in a sling, and played a Copa del Rey final with a broken jaw!

MESUT OZIL

SEASONS: 2010-13

Ozil is one of the most unselfish, creative players of all time, and he showcased that perfectly during his three seasons at the Bernabeu. He topped their assists chart every year, bagging 94 in total for club and country while playing in Spain!

BEST OF THE REST... CHECK OUT THESE OTHER SUPERSTARS!

FERNANDO REDONDO
Seasons: 1994-2000

MIGUEL MUNOZ
Seasons: 1948-58

LUKA MODRIC
Seasons: 2012-Present

IGNACIO ZOCO
Seasons: 1962-74

GUTI
Seasons: 1995-2010

TONI KROOS

SEASONS: 2014-PRESENT

When Xabi Alonso left the Bernabeu, Real fans were sad to see a legend leave, but they weren't worried because his replacement had just been signed! Kroos has exactly the same levels of composure and eagle-eyed vision for a pass!

ZINEDINE ZIDANE

SEASONS: 2001-06

Before he became a legend in the dugout, Zizou was a hero on the pitch. He didn't just win everything, he did it with a level of skill that most players can only dream of – and a style that made every game he played worth watching!

VICENTE DEL BOSQUE

SEASONS: 1968-84

Del Bosque won two CLs and the World Cup as a gaffer, but he first made his name bossing Los Blancos' midfield! In over 440 La Liga games he lifted the title five times, and played in a famous 4-0 win against Barcelona in the Copa del Rey final!

XABI ALONSO

SEASONS: 2009-14

Alonso is recognised as one of the best passers of his generation – he could keep it simple and play possession football, or hit long balls with incredible accuracy. He won loads at Real and also bagged 114 international caps for Spain!

STEVE McMANAMAN

SEASONS: 1999-2003

McManaman moved to the Bernabeu on a free transfer from his hometown club Liverpool, and it turned out to be a brilliant piece of business. In his first season, he scored a beautifully-struck volley in the Champions League final!

BEST OF THE REST... CHECK OUT THESE OTHER SUPERSTARS!

ANGEL DI MARIA

Seasons: 2010-14

ISCO

Seasons: 2013- Present

KAKA

Seasons: 2009-13

MICHEL

Seasons: 1982-96

NOW PICK YOUR ALL-TIME REAL MADRID DREAM TEAM MIDFIELDERS!

TURN TO PAGE 42

CRISTIANO RONALDO

SEASONS: 2009–2018

With every record-breaking season Cristiano completed at Real, he cemented his claim as the club's greatest of all time. Not only did he overtake Raul's all-time goalscoring record of 323 in 2015, he did it in 431 fewer games!

RAYMOND KOPA

SEASONS: 1956-59

Kopa's one of just six players to win the Ballon d'Or at Real! The winger was signed by Madrid after showing off his dazzling ability against them in the 1956 European Cup final, and he went on to win the next three trophies with the Spanish giants!

RONALDO

SEASONS: 2002-07

Many players have won more trophies at Real than Ronaldo, but very few were as talented as him. On top form, 'The Phenomenon' was absolutely unstoppable – he scored 30 goals in each of his first two seasons at the Bernabeu!

FERENC PUSKAS

SEASONS: 1958-67

Puskas' movement totally baffled defenders and when he got into space he rarely missed! The Hungary striker's deadly left foot fired him to four Pichichis in five years, and he's the only player ever to score four goals in a European Cup final!

SANTILLANA

SEASONS: 1971-88

In Real's record books, this guy's name crops up a lot! The Spaniard is fourth on both the club's list of top scorers and appearance makers, and has played more Copa del Rey games than any Real player too. In total, he won 16 trophies with Los Blancos and scored 290 times!

BEST OF THE REST...
CHECK OUT THESE OTHER SUPERSTARS!

HUGO SANCHEZ
Seasons: 1985-92

GARETH BALE
Seasons: 2013-Present

AMANCIO AMARO
Seasons: 1962-76

KARIM BENZEMA
Seasons: 2009-Present

FERNANDO MORIENTES
Seasons: 1997-2005

ALFREDO DI STEFANO

SEASONS: 1953-64

Before Cristiano Ronaldo, Di Stefano was widely regarded as Real Madrid's greatest player of all time – and to many he still is! He scored in five European Cup finals too – he's the only player ever to do that in the competition's history!

PREDRAG MIJATOVIC

SEASONS: 1996-99

Mijatovic only spent a short time at Real, but he had a huge impact. He fired them to the title in his first season, and the following year hit the winner in the 1998 Champions League final v Juventus – ending their 32-year wait for the trophy!

RAUL

SEASONS: 1994-2010

While most of Raul's team-mates were expensive Galacticos from around the world, the home-grown hero was probably Madrid's most important player. He scored in two CL finals, and left the club holding the goal and appearances records!

FRANCISCO GENTO

SEASONS: 1953-71

As the only man ever to win six European Cups, Gento is an all-time great. The Spaniard played on the left of Real's ace attack starring Puskas, Di Stefano and Kopa, and terrorised defenders with his pace, dribbling and lethal left foot!

LUIS FIGO

SEASONS: 2000-05

Figo had been ripping up La Liga for years at Barça before joining Real for a world-record £37.2 million! The Portugal legend was the perfect winger – his mega fast feet, demon dribbling and accurate crossing earned him the 2000 Ballon d'Or!

BEST OF THE REST... CHECK OUT THESE OTHER SUPERSTARS!

RUUD VAN NISTELROOY
Seasons: 2006-10

IVAN ZAMORANO
Seasons: 1992-96

EMILIO BUTRAGUENO
Seasons: 1982-95

GONZALO HIGUAIN
Seasons: 2007-13

NOW PICK YOUR ALL-TIME REAL MADRID DREAM TEAM FORWARDS!

TURN OVER

DREAM TEAM
MY ALL-TIME REAL XI!

The Perfect team
made up of man city &
aberdeen

You've seen MATCH's all-time Madrid shortlist, now pick your fave starting XI!

GOALKEEPER
Jerry Jemus

RIGHT-BACK
gream Shinne

CENTRE-BACK
Stones

CENTRE-BACK
mcenna

LEFT-BACK
Walker

MIDFIELDER
Kevindebruyne

MIDFIELDER
Leroy Sane

MIDFIELDER
kareem sterling

FORWARD
Emmy

FORWARD
Sam Cosgrove

FORWARD
auger

WIN! A REAL 2018-19 KIDS HOME SHIRT!

SPORTS DIRECT

Pick your favourite team and if it's the same as MATCH's all-time Real Madrid XI, you'll be put into the draw! One lucky reader will then be picked at random to win a 2018-19 Real Madrid kids home shirt, thanks to our top mates at Sports Direct. Get entering now!

Just fill in your Dream Team and details, then send a photocopy of this page to: Real Madrid Dream Team 2019, MATCH Magazine, Kelsey Media, Regent House, Welbeck Way, Peterborough, Cambridgeshire, PE2 7WH

Closing date: January 31, 2019.

Name: Emmy

Date of birth: 06/01/19

Address: 3 abernethy View

Mobile: 07743 6308

Email: Lorrain tomb @ Emily hotto

Kids shirt size: 9-10

THE MAD MADRIDISTAS!

MATCH takes a look at what it really means to be a Real Madrid fan!

Most of Real Madrid's cool nicknames are all about their kit colour – from 'Los Blancos', The Whites to 'Los Merengues', The Meringues – but the fans simply call themselves Madridistas, because the team represents their city!

HALA MADRID

After winning 'La Decima', their tenth CL trophy, Real released a new club anthem called 'Hala Madrid y Nada Mas' – Come On Madrid and Nothing More!

The history you've made
The history you'll make!
Because no-one can resist
Your willingness to win!

The stars are now coming out!
My old Chamartin...
From far away and from nearby
you gather us all here!

I wear your shirt
right next to my heart!
The days you play
are everything I am!

The Arrow is running!
My Madrid is attacking!

I am struggle! I am beauty!
The cry I learned:

Madrid! Madrid! Madrid!
Hala Madrid!

And nothing more!
And nothing more!
Hala Madrid!

MADRIDISTA CHECKLIST
See how many of these you can tick off!

Get snapped in a Real Madrid shirt! ✓

Take a tour of the Bernabeu museum!

Watch the stars arrive for a game in their cars!

Cheer them on at a match in the Bernabeu!

Follow all the players on Instagram!

Stick a Real hero MATCH poster on your wall! ✓

Practise and perfect the Zidane Roulette!

Beat Barcelona 5-0 in a friendly on FIFA! ✓

Learn the tune to 'Hala Madrid' – see right! ✓

You Tube

Scan the QR code to give it a listen and follow what the victorious players sung!

43

STAT ATTACK!

Get a load of **REAL MADRID**'s biggest signings, trophy cabinet, record scorers, appearance makers and loads more!

FIVE BIGGEST SIGNINGS

	PLAYER	YEAR	FEE
1	Gareth Bale	2013	£85.3m
2	Cristiano Ronaldo	2009	£80m
3	James Rodríguez	2014	£63m
4	Kaka	2009	£56m
5	Zinedine Zidane	2001	£46m

FIVE BIGGEST SALES

	PLAYER	YEAR	FEE
1	Cristiano Ronaldo	2018	£99.2m
2	Alvaro Morata	2017	£60m
3	Angel Di Maria	2014	£59.7m
4	Mesut Ozil	2013	£42.5m
5	Gonzalo Higuain	2013	£34.5m

MAJOR TROPHIES

13 Champions League

3 FIFA Club World Cup

3 Intercontinental Cup

2 Europa League

4 European Super Cup

33 La Liga

19 Copa del Rey

11 Spanish Super Cup

MOST APPEARANCES

Player	Years	Apps
Raul	1994–2010	741
Iker Casillas	1999–2015	725
Manuel Sanchis	1983–2001	710
Santillana	1971–1988	645
Fernando Hierro	1989–2003	601
Francisco Gento	1953–1971	601
Jose Camacho	1973–1989	577
Sergio Ramos	2005–present	565
Pirri	1964–1980	561
Michel	1981–1996	559

12

Chilean striker Ivan Zamorano scored after just 12 seconds against Sevilla in 1994 – the fastest goal in Real's history!

CHAMPIONS LEAGUE RECORD

ALL-TIME

PLAYED	WON
251	**151**

LOST	DRAWN
51	**49**

GOALS	CONCEDED
536	**271**

121

Real once went a record 121 games unbeaten at home – a streak lasting over eight years! In 2011–12, they also scored 121 goals in the most prolific La Liga season ever!

ALL-TIME TOP SCORERS

- Emilio Butragueno 171
- Pirri 172
- Cristiano Ronaldo 450
- Francisco Gento 182
- Raul 323
- Karim Benzema 193
- Alfredo Di Stefano 308
- Hugo Sanchez 208
- Santillana 290
- Ferenc Puskas 242

22

Real have participated in 22 Champions League campaigns – no team has played in more!

13

Number of Real Madrid Pichichi winners!

Manuel Olivares 1933	Juanito 1984	Ronaldo 2004
Pahino 1952	Hugo Sanchez 1986, 1987, 1988 & 1990	Ruud van Nistelrooy 2007
Alfredo Di Stefano 1954, 1956, 1957, 1958 & 1959	Emilio Butragueno 1991	Cristiano Ronaldo 2011, 2014 & 2015
Ferenc Puskas 1960, 1961, 1963 & 1964	Ivan Zamorano 1995	
Amancio 1969 & 1970	Raul 1999 & 2001	

YOUNGEST & OLDEST PLAYERS

MARTIN ODEGAARD

16

16 years & 157 days
v Getafe, 2015

FERENC PUSKAS

38

38 years and 233 days
v Sevilla, 1965

facebook

109+ MILLION Likes

59+ MILLION Likes

twitter

30+ MILLION Likes

Stats only include official matches. Correct up to start of the 2018-19 season.

REAL'S RECORD BREAKERS!

Meet the men who have broken world records at the Bernabeu!

IKER CASILLAS

Spain's World Cup 2010 winning captain won 162 caps while playing for Real, and has won more La Liga games than any other player too!

Champions League matches	167
Champions League clean sheets	58
Total Spain caps	167
La Liga wins	334

ALFREDO DI STEFANO

Di Stefano didn't miss a league game for almost six years, and is the only man to score in five different European Cup finals!

Consecutive La Liga games	171
Goals in European Cup finals	7

FERENC PUSKAS

Puskas is tied with his old team-mate Di Stefano for most goals in European Cup finals, but he's the only man to score four in one!

Goals in European Cup finals	7

PACO GENTO

One of the most successful Spanish footballers of all time was ever-present during Real's glory years of the 1950s and '60s!

La Liga title wins	12
European Cup wins	6

SERGIO RAMOS

Sergio Ramos is legendary for loads of good reasons, but also for his shocking disciplinary record!

La Liga red cards	18
Champions League yellow cards	35

RAUL

Raul was the Champions League's all-time top scorer before Lionel Messi and Cristiano Ronaldo came along, but is still a La Liga legend!

La Liga games with one club	550

CRISTIANO RONALDO

Ronaldo totally destroyed Champions League and La Liga goalscoring records for Real between 2009 and 2018!

Champions League goals	**120**	Champions League assists	**34**
Champions League goals in a season	**17**	La Liga hat-tricks	**34**
Champions League Golden Boots	**7**	La Liga penalties	**61**
Champions League hat-tricks	**7**	Ballon d'Or awards	**5**

TRANSFER RECORD BREAKERS!

Real have broken the world transfer record five times – more than any other club!

2000
Luis Figo

From Barcelona
£37.2 million

2001
Zinedine Zidane

From Juventus
£46 million

2009
Kaka

From AC Milan
£56 million

2009
Cristiano Ronaldo

From Man. United
£80 million

2013
Gareth Bale

From Tottenham
£85.3 million

CROSSWORD

Use the clues to complete this tricky Real Madrid crossword!

ACROSS

3. Nickname for Real's mega clash with Barcelona! (2,7)

6. Surname of Real Madrid's wicked Welsh winger! (4)

7. Santiago _ _ _ _ _ _ _ _ – the man Madrid named their stadium after! (8)

10. Legendary Hungarian forward, Ferenc _ _ _ _ _ _! (6)

11. Fernando _ _ _ _ _ _ – former captain who won three CLs with Real! (6)

12. Legendary Spanish striker who scored more than 300 goals for Real! (4)

15. Wicked national team that midfield superstar Luka Modric plays for! (7)

17. German club that Real signed Dani Carvajal from back in 2013! (5,10)

18. Italian stadium where Real won their eleventh Champions League trophy back in 2016! (3,4)

19. Former Real Madrid and England striker! (7,4)

20. Lethal Brazilian striker who joined Real from Inter for mega bucks in 2002! (7)

DOWN

1. English club which Real signed Cristiano Ronaldo from in 2009! (10,6)

2. Famous Italian side that lost to Real in the 2017 Champions League Final! (8)

4. Real's wicked nickname, which translates from Spanish to 'The Whites'! (3,7)

5. Defender and current Real Madrid captain! (6,5)

8. Name of the Real Madrid 'B' team, which plays in the Segunda Division B! (8)

9. Morocco ace who's on loan at Borussia Dortmund from the Spanish giants! (6,6)

13. Squad number of Brazil left-back Marcelo! (6)

14. Brazilian club that lost to Real in the 2017 FIFA Club World Cup Final! (6)

16. Norwegian wonderkid and Real Madrid's youngest ever footballer aged just 16, Martin _ _ _ _ _ _ _ _! (8)

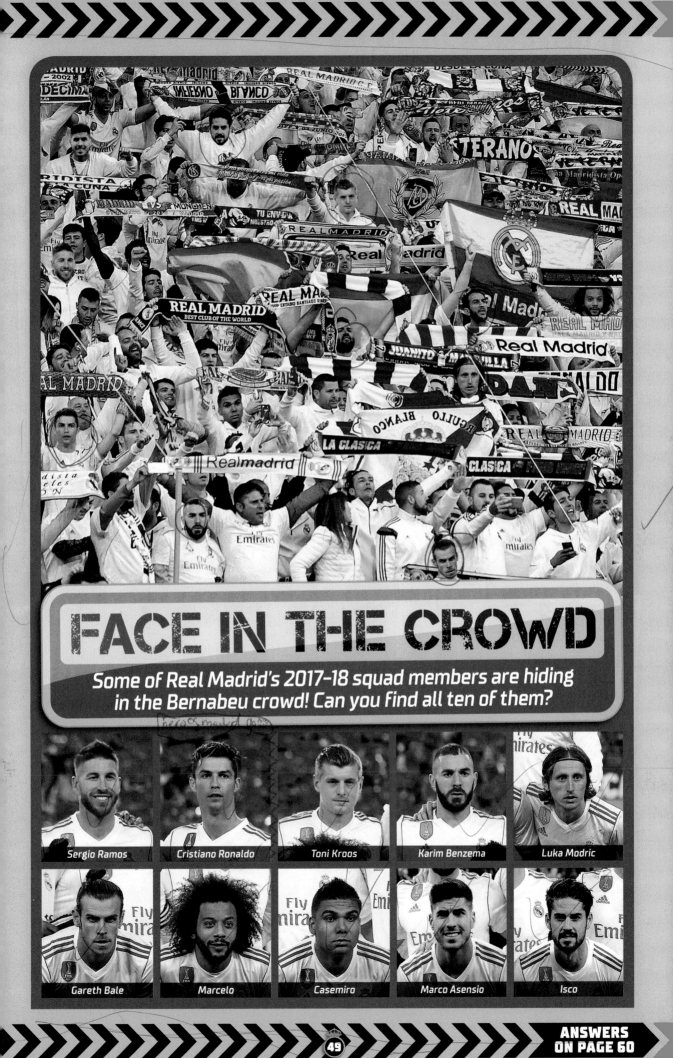

FACE IN THE CROWD

Some of Real Madrid's 2017-18 squad members are hiding in the Bernabeu crowd! Can you find all ten of them?

Sergio Ramos
Cristiano Ronaldo
Toni Kroos
Karim Benzema
Luka Modric
Gareth Bale
Marcelo
Casemiro
Marco Asensio
Isco

ANSWERS ON PAGE 60

REAL MADRID

RECORD BREAKER

July 2001

In the summer of 2001, Zidane was the best footballer on the planet. He'd fired France to the 1998 World Cup and Euro 2000, and been named FIFA's World Player of the Year twice. Real Madrid paid Juventus a world-record transfer fee of £46 million, yet it turned out to be a bargain!

CLASICO KING

April 2002

The 2002 CL semi-finals made history by drawing Real against Barça for the first time since the competition's re-format. In the first leg at the Nou Camp Zidane was the hero, opening the scoring for Los Blancos in a 2-0 win to send them on their way to the final!

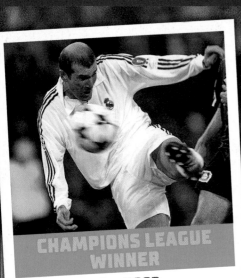

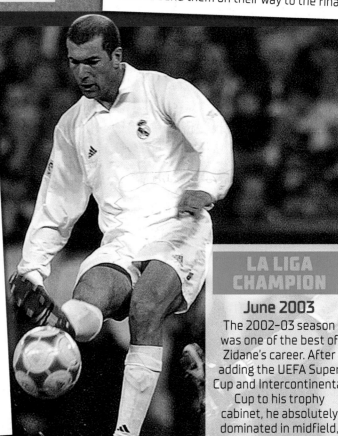

CHAMPIONS LEAGUE WINNER

May 2002

Zidane ended his first season in Spain with seven La Liga goals and was named the league's best foreign player, but his best moment came in the Champions League final. The French wizard struck a sensational volley from the edge of the box to seal a 2-1 win – arguably the greatest ever goal in a CL final!

LA LIGA CHAMPION

June 2003

The 2002-03 season was one of the best of Zidane's career. After adding the UEFA Super Cup and Intercontinental Cup to his trophy cabinet, he absolutely dominated in midfield, scoring nine goals, and lifting the La Liga title!

scrapbook!

Zizou shocked the world by leaving Real after winning a third Champo League as gaffer in 2018. Check out his career with the Spanish club!

WORLD'S BEST

December 2003

A brilliant year for Zidane ended in the perfect way, as he became only the second star to be named FIFA World Player of the Year for the third time, beating fellow Frenchman Thierry Henry and Real Madrid team-mate Ronaldo to the award!

BYE-BYE, ZIZOU

May 2006

Zidane announced his plans to retire from football after the 2006 World Cup, and he scored in his final match for Real. His team-mates wore shirts with 'ZIDANE 2001-2006' on them and 80,000 supporters gave him a magical send-off, but his international career ended in disaster – he was sent off for a bonkers headbutt in the World Cup final defeat to Italy!

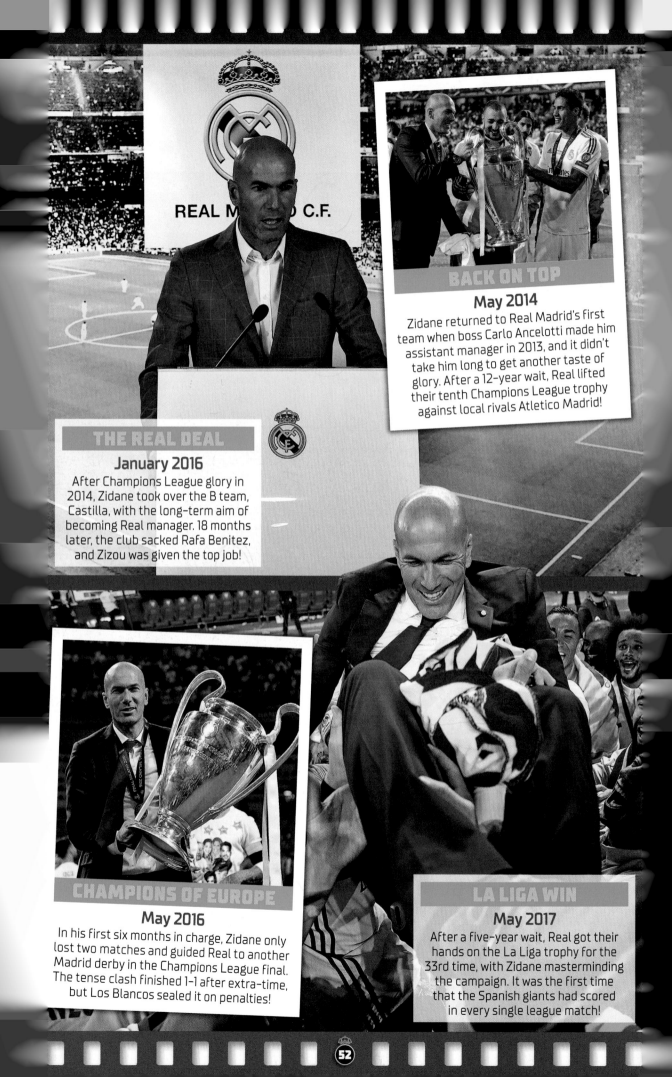

BACK ON TOP

May 2014

Zidane returned to Real Madrid's first team when boss Carlo Ancelotti made him assistant manager in 2013, and it didn't take him long to get another taste of glory. After a 12-year wait, Real lifted their tenth Champions League trophy against local rivals Atletico Madrid!

THE REAL DEAL

January 2016

After Champions League glory in 2014, Zidane took over the B team, Castilla, with the long-term aim of becoming Real manager. 18 months later, the club sacked Rafa Benitez, and Zizou was given the top job!

CHAMPIONS OF EUROPE

May 2016

In his first six months in charge, Zidane only lost two matches and guided Real to another Madrid derby in the Champions League final. The tense clash finished 1-1 after extra-time, but Los Blancos sealed it on penalties!

LA LIGA WIN

May 2017

After a five-year wait, Real got their hands on the La Liga trophy for the 33rd time, with Zidane masterminding the campaign. It was the first time that the Spanish giants had scored in every single league match!

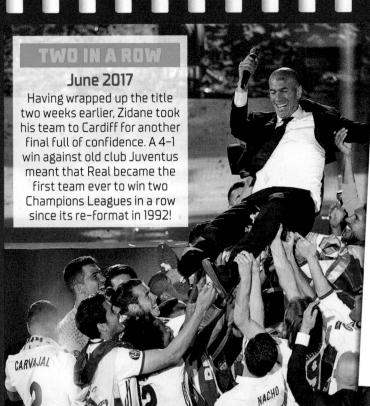

TWO IN A ROW
June 2017

Having wrapped up the title two weeks earlier, Zidane took his team to Cardiff for another final full of confidence. A 4-1 win against old club Juventus meant that Real became the first team ever to win two Champions Leagues in a row since its re-format in 1992!

SUPERCOPA WIN
August 2017

Zidane only had one Clasico win under his manager's belt before the start of the 2017-18 season, but he ended that record in style with a 5-1 aggregate victory over Barcelona. After lifting the Spanish Super Cup, the boss had almost won as many trophies as he'd lost matches!

THREE IN A ROW
May 2018

Just like his playing career, Zidane ended his time as boss at the highest stage, but this time there were no red cards, and no disappointments. The only downside after the 3-1 Champions League final victory over Liverpool was Gareth Bale challenging his title of best ever CL final goal!

TOP 5... REAL RIVALS!

You can't be the biggest club in the world without attracting some massive footy enemies! Check out Real Madrid's top five rivals...

5 BAYERN MUNICH

Nobody's played more times in the Champo League than Real and Bayern, so they've built up a huge rivalry over the years. Last season saw the 20th meeting between the teams in the competition since its re-format in 1992, and all but two of the clashes have been in the knockout stages!

HEAD-TO-HEAD

Real Wins	12	Draws	3	Bayern Wins	11

VILLAIN
MANUEL NEUER

Real were chasing a tenth CL title and their first for ten years v Bayern in the 2012 semis. With Los Blancos dreaming of La Decima, their hopes were crushed by the keeper – first in normal time, then with two saves in the penalty shootout!

HERO
CRISTIANO RONALDO

Ronaldo's record against Bayern underlined just how much he delivered on the big stage for Real. In eight matches against the German giants, he scored nine times, including five in the 2016-17 CL semi-finals en route to the trophy!

4 ATHLETIC BILBAO

There's a good reason why this clash is known as 'The Old Clasico'. Real first met Bilbao in 1903 and, as two of only three teams to have played in every La Liga season, they've clashed loads of times. The Basques are always desperate to get one over the capital club, but Real usually come out on top.

HEAD-TO-HEAD

Real Wins	114	Draws	42	Athletic Wins	75

VILLAIN
ASIER DEL HORNO

Striker Dani was the villain in the 1980s, but an uncanny enemy in the 2000s was left-back Del Horno. He only scored 13 La Liga goals for Bilbao – but five of them came against Real, and they came in three shock wins – one of which was at the Bernabeu!

HERO
FERENC PUSKAS

The Hungary forward was a goal king in the 1950s and 1960s, and he loved netting against Bilbao. In 12 league matches, Puskas hit 11 goals, never lost, and was on target against Athletic in all five of Real's title-winning seasons from 1961 to 1965!

3 MAN. UNITED

Real Madrid's rivalry with United is just as much about matters off the pitch as on it. The two super clubs regularly battle it out at the top of footy's rich list, and have gone head-to-head over tons of players – from David Beckham and Cristiano Ronaldo, to David de Gea and Paul Pogba!

HEAD-TO-HEAD

Real Wins	5	Draws	4	United Wins	2

VILLAIN
DAVID DE GEA

The ex-Atletico GK put in some top displays in Madrid derbies, and continues to frustrate Real's attackers for United. The Spain No.1 was set to join Real in 2015, but a mysterious error with a fax machine prevented the paper work being completed in time!

HERO
RONALDO

It takes a very special opponent to be applauded off the pitch at Old Trafford, but that's what happened to Ronaldo when he single-handedly destroyed The Red Devils' defence in 2003. His sick hat-trick dumped United out of the CL quarter-finals!

2 ATLETICO MADRID

The Madrid giants have been fierce rivals for over 90 years, and while Real have bossed it in terms of wins and trophies, Atleti are now real challengers. The rivalry peaked in 2016 when they met in their second CL final in three seasons, but Atletico had to watch on as their rivals lifted the trophy again.

HEAD-TO-HEAD

Real Wins	109	Draws	55	Atletico Wins	55

VILLAIN
DIEGO SIMEONE

Atletico spent most of their history in Real's shadow until Diego arrived as boss. He turned them into title challengers, ending a 14-year winless run against Real to lift the 2013 Copa del Rey, before beating them to the 2013-14 La Liga title.

HERO
RAUL

Only CR7 and Di Stefano have hit more goals for Real in the Madrid derby than Raul's total of 15. He started out in Atleti's academy, but after it was closed to save money, he joined Real. It proved to be one of the costliest errors they've ever made.

1 BARCELONA

The biggest rivalry in footy needs no introduction! When Spain's most successful clubs face-off, it's watched all over the world – and usually decides who'll win trophies too. Barça may have lifted the title in 2018, but Real are still on top when it comes to total La Liga and Champions League victories!

HEAD-TO-HEAD

Real Wins	95	Draws	50	Barça Wins	92

VILLAIN
LIONEL MESSI

If Leo had never left Argentina as a teenager, Spanish footy history would be very different! El Clasico's all-time top scorer has been a thorn in Real's side for years, dumping them out of the 2011 CL semis, and firing Barça to nine La Liga titles!

HERO
ALFREDO DI STEFANO

Di Stefano is Real's joint-top scorer in El Clasicos, and he'll always be a hero in Madrid and hated in Barça. The forward was part of a massive transfer tussle between the two clubs in 1953, before going on to score 18 goals v the Nou Camp club!

VARANE

THE COMPLETE DEFENDER

The World Cup-winning CB will boss strikers for years to come.

If scientists tried to build the perfect centre-back, it would probably look a lot like Real Madrid superstar Raphael Varane. A natural athlete blessed with a top football brain, super strength, lightning speed and an incredible leap, the France defender reads the game like a book and passes the ball out from defence like he's a midfielder. When it comes to one-on-one battles with strikers, he's almost impossible to beat – whether it's simply shrugging them off with his power, quickly intercepting possession or perfectly timing a tackle. At the age of 25, he's not short of experience either, with more than 60 Champions League games and two World Cups for France under his belt. With a massive collection of trophies too, there's nothing to stop Varane from going on to become one of the greatest defenders of all time.

MADRID COME CALLING

Just 24 games for French club Lens was all that it took to convince Real to swoop for Varane. At the end of his debut season in 2011, the Spanish giants paid just under £9 million to bring the then 18-year-old to the Bernabeu, although he took some persuading. When Zinedine Zidane called to try to seal the transfer, Raphael replied, "I'm a bit busy at the moment, can you call me another time?"

THE REAL DEAL

Real Madrid won the La Liga title in Varane's first season at the club. Although he only played nine games, he was unbeaten in them – winning eight – while in September he became the club's youngest ever foreign scorer aged 18 years and 152 days. By the end of the season, he had proven himself as a Madrid player and over the next two years developed into one of the world's top defenders.

CHAMPO LEAGUE CHAMP

In 2014, Varane started the Champions League final against Atletico Madrid as the youngest player on the pitch, but played like a veteran to help guide Real to victory. Only injury prevented him from appearing in the rematch two years later, but he returned for both the 2017 and 2018 victories. No Frenchman has won the trophy more times and there are surely more to come.

WORLD CUP WINNER

Fresh from European glory, Varane headed to Russia 2018 as France's first-choice centre-back and showed the world why he's so loved by the Real fans. The beastly defender didn't miss a single minute of Les Bleus' run to the trophy, producing some faultless displays, and became only the fourth player to lift the Champions League and World Cup trophies in the same year.

TROPHY CABINET

1x World Cup

4x Champions Leagues

2x La Ligas

3x Club World Cups

1x Copa del Rey

3x European Super Cups

2x Spanish Super Cups

2018-19 FIRST TEAM SQUAD

GOALKEEPERS

No.	Player		La Liga Games/Goals 2017-18	Signed from
1	Keylor Navas		27/0	Levante, 2014
13	Kiko Casilla		10/0	Espanyol, 2015
25	Thibaut Courtois		N/A	Chelsea, 2018
30	Luca Zidane		1/0	Academy

Courtois

DEFENDERS

No.	Player		La Liga Games/Goals 2017-18	Signed from
2	Dani Carvajal		25/0	B. Leverkusen, 2013
3	Jesus Vallejo		7/0	Real Zaragoza, 2015
4	Sergio Ramos		26/4	Sevilla, 2005
5	Raphael Varane		27/0	Lens, 2011
6	Nacho		27/3	Academy
12	Marcelo		28/2	Fluminense, 2007
19	Alvaro Odriozola		35/0	Real Sociedad, 2018
23	Sergio Reguilon		N/A	Academy

Odriozola

MIDFIELDERS

No.	Player		La Liga Games/Goals 2017-18	Signed from
8	Toni Kroos		27/5	Bayern Munich, 2014
10	Luka Modric		26/1	Tottenham, 2012
14	Casemiro		30/5	Sao Paulo, 2013
15	Federico Valverde		24/0	Academy
18	Marcos Llorente		13/0	Academy
20	Marco Asensio		32/6	Mallorca, 2014
22	Isco		30/7	Malaga, 2013
24	Dani Ceballos		12/2	Real Betis, 2017

Vinicus Jr.

FORWARDS

No.	Player		La Liga Games/Goals 2017-18	Signed from
7	Mariano		N/A	Lyon, 2018
9	Karim Benzema		32/5	Lyon, 2009
11	Gareth Bale		26/16	Tottenham, 2013
17	Lucas Vazquez		33/4	Academy
28	Vinicius Jr.		N/A	Flamengo, 2018

MEET THE MANAGER...

JULEN LOPETEGUI

Country: Spain

D.O.B: 28 August, 1966

Former Team: Spain

Honours: 1x European Under-19 Championship, 1x European Under-21 Championship

"Yesterday was the worst day of my life, but today is the happiest day of my life." Julen Lopetegui was named Real Madrid manager on 12 June, 2018 under a cloud. Having agreed to take over the European champions just days before the 2018 World Cup kicked off in Russia, the Spanish FA wasted no time in sacking him as national coach. The next day, he was in Madrid for his first press conference with his new club.

The ex-Spain goalkeeper was back at the Bernabeu for the third time in his career. He first joined Real Madrid in 1985, playing more than 60 times for their B-team Castilla, before going on to appear for Las Palmas, Logrones, Barcelona and Rayo Vallecano, but his future was always in coaching.

Since retiring from playing in 2002, he's coached the Spanish youth teams from the Under-17s up to the Under-21s, as well as Rayo Vallecano, Castilla, Porto and the senior national team. Now after landing his dream job, he'll be hoping for more happy days and lots of trophies to come.

Wordsearch — P16

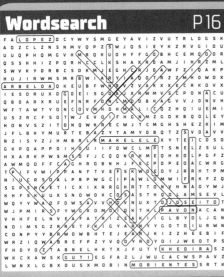

Brain-Buster — P30

1. 1902
2. Marco Asensio
3. Costa Rica
4. False
5. Iker Casillas
6. Gareth Bale
7. 22
8. True
9. Borussia Dortmund
10. Malaga

Name The Team — P17

1. Keylor Navas
2. Sergio Ramos
3. Toni Kroos
4. Casemiro
5. Karim Benzema
6. Raphael Varane
7. Gareth Bale
8. Marcelo
9. Dani Carvajal
10. Isco
11. Luka Modric

Spot The Difference — P31

Crossword — P48

Across/Down:
- EL CLASICO
- JUVENTUS
- BALE
- BERNABEU
- PUSKAS
- HIERRO
- RAUL
- CROATIA
- BAYERLEVERKUSEN
- SANSIRO
- MICHAELOWEN
- RONALDO

Face In The Crowd — P49

LOVE MATCH?
GET IT DELIVERED EVERY WEEK!

MEGA GIFTS

COOL PANINI STICKERS 5 STICKERS IN A PACK!

WORLD CUP 3 WEEKS TO GO!

MATCH!

CL FINAL SPECIAL!

RONALDO V SALAH!

CHAMPO LEAGUE FINAL SHOWDOWN!

TEKELA New boot revealed!

KIT ALERT! Bayern Munich, Man. City & Crystal Palace strips!

INTERVIEWS ▶ TRANSFER GOSSIP

4 ISSUES FOR JUST £1!*

PACKED EVERY WEEK WITH...

★ Red-hot gear

★ FIFA tips

★ Stats & quizzes

★ Massive stars

★ Posters & pics

& loads more!

HOW TO SUBSCRIBE TO MATCH!

CALL 📱
01959 543 747
QUOTE: MAT400

ONLINE 🖱
SHOP.KELSEY.CO.UK/ MAT400

ROLL OF HONOUR

FIFA CLUB OF THE CENTURY
2000

CHAMPIONS LEAGUE
1955–56, 1956–57, 1957–58, 1958–59, 1959–60, 1965–66, 1997–98, 1999–2000, 2001–02, 2013–14, 2015–16, 2016–17, 2017–18

FIFA CLUB WORLD CUP
2014, 2016, 2017

INTERCONTINENTAL CUP
1960, 1998, 2002

UEFA CUP
1984–85, 1985–86

EUROPEAN SUPER CUP
2002, 2014, 2016, 2017

LA LIGA
1931–32, 1932–33, 1953–54, 1954–55, 1956–57, 1957–58, 1960–61, 1961–62, 1962–63, 1963–64, 1964–65, 1966–67, 1967–68, 1968–69, 1971–72, 1974–75, 1975–76, 1977–78, 1978–79, 1979–80, 1985–86, 1986–87, 1987–88, 1988–89, 1989–90, 1994–95, 1996–97, 2000–01, 2002–03, 2006–07, 2007–08, 2011–12, 2016–17

COPA DEL REY
1904–05, 1905–06, 1906–07, 1907–08, 1916–17, 1933–34, 1935–36, 1945–46, 1946–47, 1961–62, 1969–70, 1973–74, 1974–75, 1979–80, 1981–82, 1988–89, 1992–93, 2010–11, 2013–14

SPANISH SUPER CUP
1988, 1989, 1990, 1993, 1997, 2001, 2003, 2008, 2012, 2017

SPANISH LEAGUE CUP
1984–85

SMALL WORLD CUP
1952, 1956

LATIN CUP
1955, 1957

REGIONAL CHAMPIONSHIP
1903–04, 1904–05, 1905–06, 1906–07, 1907–08, 1912–13, 1915–16, 1916–17, 1917–18, 1919–20, 1921–22, 1922–23, 1923–24, 1925–26, 1926–27, 1928–29, 1929–30, 1930–31

MANCOMUNADOS TROPHY
1931–32, 1932–33, 1933–34, 1934–35, 1935–36

COPA IBEROAMERICANA
1994

COPA EVA DUARTE
1947